The Crimson Tome

THE CRIMSON TOME

K. A. Opperman

Foreword by Dr. W. C. Farmer

Introduction by Donald Sidney-Fryer

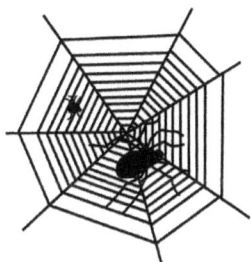

Hippocampus Press

New York

Acknowledgments: see p. 182.

Published by Hippocampus Press
P.O. Box 641, New York, NY 10156
http://www.hippocampuspress.com

Cover design by Barbara Briggs Silbert.
Hippocampus Press logo designed by Anastasia Damianakos.

First Edition
1 3 5 7 9 8 6 4 2

ISBN 978-1-61498-132-9

Contents

Preface: Opperman's Opus

In the nearly sixty years since I became a close personal friend of pioneering poet and author Clark Ashton Smith, I have waited patiently watching a sleeping world rediscover the "Keats of the Sierras." For several years now, through the Internet, websites, and new publications we have seen a resurgence of interest in the genre he almost single-handedly founded. Now, at last, my vigil has been rewarded.

I believe I can state unequivocally, and on whatever authority may cling to the fact of being Smith's last living close personal friend, that the torch has been passed to a new generation. No mere clone, Mr. Opperman brings a freshness to this esoteric genre that burns with a freshened fire—his compelling verse, and skill as a poet, using the tools with an artistry beyond his years, gives evidence of present mastery that promises to take his readers "further in, and farther up" within the Deep Magic.

Occasional subtle humor rides seamlessly woven within a dark sonority that has surprising power, like the thirty-two-foot bass pedal on a great organ, yet rising within an unexpected moment that can almost be called "redemptive." This work should not be dipped into here and there, but treated like a prelude and fugue played without interruption to its faultless summation. Read this fine work—then return to read the introduction and preface again—and stand back in wonder.

All will be made clear.

—DR. W. C. FARMER

Introduction:
Crimson Pages from the Future Perfect Past

Once upon a time a certain remarkable pulp magazine existed by the name of *Weird Tales,* and sustained that existence from 1923 to 1954. Certain writers and poets contributed to "The Unique Magazine" (as the subtitle ran). Although similar as well as dissimilar in background and education, as observed in the fantastic, often macabre stories that they had published in it, they had enough similarities to merit the term of a "*Weird Tales* School." The late L. Sprague de Camp, fictioneer, popularizer, and critic, rightfully considered them "the Three [or four] Musketeers of *Weird Tales*": Henry S. Whitehead, H. P. Lovecraft, Robert E. Howard, and Clark Ashton Smith. Other scriveners came along somewhat later to add their own distinction to the periodical: E. Hoffmann Price, August Derleth, Manly Wade Wellman, Seabury Quinn, Ray Bradbury, etc.

Arkham House under August Derleth later gathered many of their stories into a series of handsome hardcover books, either anthologies or collections devoted to one author or another. These books in turn gave entertainment and inspiration to new generations of readers and budding authors. Thus, despite the initial inattention or even disdain meted out to the magazine by the literary mainstream, the best stories by these authors have obviously survived to become canonical classics. However, the poets inspired by them, especially those working in traditional forms, have appeared but few and far between.

A new poet, and a traditionalist (albeit innovative), has now made his appearance to augment the limited register of these poets' names. He is K. A. Opperman, and he makes his debut with the volume in hand. Given the almost relentless pageant of doom and gloom, of death and blood, invoked herein, one would never guess that the author of this poetry is not some cynical, world-weary, and pessimistic older man, but instead a bright and agreeable young adult in his mid-twenties.

And just what has Opperman presented in his first collection to the aficionado of fantastic and/or macabre poetry? Overall *The Crimson Tome* contains six sections, or more properly, six collections. His first auctorial offering is a collection of collections. In the order of presentation these include: *The Nightmare Muse, Unpleasant Dreams, Nocturnal Lovers: I, Nocturnal Lovers: II, The Palace of Phantasies,* and *Twilight Sorrows.* The reader will notice that the poems often feature much beautiful and unusual (sometimes archaic) language, most of it long since abandoned, if not forbidden, by the American, but not the British, poetic mainstream.

The table of contents dutifully lists the given selections, whose titles the poet has chosen with care and cunning, titles that beguilingly invite the aficionado into their usually very dark locales, into places or situations of very grim contemplation or action. Nor does the poet fear the use of unfashionable inversions here and there; adroitly handled in general, they impart a needed elegance, emphasis, and variety. Opperman clearly knows his rhetoric, and deploys it to good effect.

Let us take a look at what the poet has offered us in this generous volume. Opperman wisely opens with a strong sonnet sequence, titled "The Land of Darkest Dreams," to some extent but not overmuch in the tradition of the *Fungi from Yuggoth* by H. P. Lovecraft, or of the *Sonnets of the Midnight Hours* by Donald Wandrei. For his own sequence Opperman has ingeniously created an unconventional sonnet slightly expanded into fifteen lines. A sonnet form in fifteen lines, what? Yes!

Before the petrifaction of the sonnet into fourteen lines, the term sonnet simply meant a "little song," its literal meaning, and could include rondeau, rondel, and other short lyric forms. An unusual and innovative rhyme arrangement—featuring an octave followed by a septet (rather than the traditional sestet)—the basic rhyme scheme appears to be, more often than not, as follows:

a b b a c b a c (octave)

d c e d e d e (septet)

Reader, have no fear! This new sonnet form works as well as any other, and surely functions quite well for Opperman. A few sonnets intriguingly mention a certain rather Lovecraftian town called Yorehaven, an apt and attractive name coined by the poet.

The next section or collection, *Unpleasant Dreams,* continues the same dark imagery and episodes, in varied forms and in length of line, such as fourteeners and alexandrines, the latter distinctly uncommon in English (apart from their use by Clark Ashton Smith and the poets of the English Symbolist school). For example, each of the seven quatrains making up "Nocturnal Poet" skillfully alternates decasyllabics with alexandrines. The poet casts "The Thirst of Count Aster" in these iambic hexameters and cleverly varies them to strong dramatic effect. Another innovation: the author has narrated "A Vampire Fear" and "Bathory" (Countess Erzsebet Bathory) in patently Swinburnian metrics, and effectively. But he also sagely avoids the diffuse indirection that can baffle and defeat the would-be reader of Swinburne's curious but individual Muse.

The two cycles of love poems constituting *Nocturnal Lovers* make an immediate impact. Despite or because of their strange mixture of the macabre with the erotic—an exceptional combination—they strike the present writer as pretty hot stuff. One admires the poet's versatility in these two notable sequences. The book's two last sections or collections, *The Palace of Phantasies* and *Twilight Sorrows,* appear as notable in their own fashion as the two connected cycles of love poems. *The Palace of Phantasies* contains among much else a powerful ballad, "Duel with the Dark Double," in which the poet combats, and vanquishes, the dark side of his own personal nature—a narrative that bears worthy comparison with some of the poetry by Robert E. Howard, that master chronicler of "sanguinary conflict" (in Lovecraft's accurate phrase), as exemplified in "The King and the Oak."

A word of warning: this volume is not for the squeamish reader. In his imagery and narrative episodes Opperman seems to delight in a crimson tide of blood (hence the Crimson Tome), not to mention an occasional flood of other precious bodily fluids. Caveat lector: let the reader beware!

Mingling metaphysical, spiritual, and physical horror, Opperman patently derives from, and meritoriously continues, the macabre heritage of the modern poetic masters in the genre (that is, of fantasy and science fiction), H. P. Lovecraft, Clark Ashton Smith, and Robert E. Howard. (Rather interestingly, all these last-named poets worked in traditional forms.) But make no mistake about it, Opperman remains very much in his own poetic persona, despite whatever he may have derived from "The Three Musketeers of *Weird Tales.*" A native Californian, he claims prominence as one of the few authors who have deliberately followed in the poetic footsteps of such Californians as Ambrose Bierce, George Sterling, and Clark Ashton Smith. As a Golden State Phantastik, K. A. Opperman in this volume becomes another original figure in the line or lineage of those unique California Romantics.

—DONALD SIDNEY-FRYER,
the Last of the Courtly Poets,
Sacramento, California

9 November 2013

THE NIGHTMARE MUSE

The Land of Darkest Dreams

I. The Nightmare Muse

The Nightmare Muse bestows her sable kiss
Upon the poet who explores the Land
Of Darkest Dreams, with dim witch-light for brand
To lead beyond the wood where shadows hiss.
Among the graves of dreamers who have died
In quest of terrors cloaked in cannabis,
The horrors of her realm are near at hand—
Hear what the monstrous mushrooms would confide. . . .

The fleeting flutter of her ebon gown
Entices those who court her as their bride.
It flaps in tempests of autumnal leaves,
To vanish in a blackness that would drown
The common seeker—for the way she weaves
Leads far away from any waking town . . .
Beyond the sphere the timid lamp perceives.

II. Yorehaven

There is an ancient, isolated town
Hemmed in by hills and woodlands without end,
Where autumn's crimson wound will never mend,
And jack-o'-lanterns all year long grin down

The Nightmare Muse

From crooked fence and sagging porch, to ward
Against the woodland wraiths that nightly wend
Along those roads that ghostly fog would drown,
With witch-light eyes that weigh each goblin gourd. . . .

A sleepiness pervades there like a spell,
And all are lost who find that haunting place—
For none have come there of their own accord,
And none may leave who in that country dwell.
Some lurking necromancy seems to lace
Yorehaven's very air—enough to quell
The strongest will to leave her strange embrace.

III. Tavern Rumors

Those who have braved the Land of Darkest Dreams,
Those who have farthest proved its ghoulish gloam,
Tell guarded rumors of a Crimson Tome—
Those who survived the moon's beguiling beams,
If but in body. . . . As for where it lies,
They only say "Beneath the night's black dome,"
Then cackle madly with strange, daemon gleams
Lighting the hollow sockets of their eyes.

Haunting Yorehaven's taverns, I have learned
Mad dreamers' secrets past all sane surmise;
But if their absinthe-tainted breath tells true,
Better had I their cryptic riddles spurned—
For they half hint that tome of crimson hue
Contains the lore of dreamers now inurned . . .
And I would share in their dark secrets, too.

IV. A Daemon Impulse

A daemon impulse whispers through my mind—
A mad compulsion tempts me to explore
The wilderness of night whose inky shore
Spills through my open window. . . . I would find
A secret way through woodlands rife with fear,
Whose labyrinthine branches bar the hoar
Rays of the stars, so tightly are they twined,
In quest of haunted dreamlands dark and drear.

Perchance this candle shall a beacon be,
If ever homeward I should live to peer,
Alike the wraith that seeks its mortal home
On Halloween, through night's eternity.
The Land of Darkest Dreams is calling me. . . .
Through midnight realms of nightmare I would roam,
In quest to find the fabled Crimson Tome.

V. The Witch-Light

I stumble through a labyrinth of black
Branches and shadows, wondering what mad
Delirium of midnight dreaming had
Made me forsake my home and not turn back.
What imp had whispered in my dreaming mind
With promise of a dark, phantasmal track
To lead me to a land forever clad
In mist and shadows that I soon must find?

The Night forbids me to forsake my quest—
For I have lost my way far, far behind.
But lo, a witch-light wakens in the night,
And I half fancy that a woman dressed
In a black gown guides me with that weird light. . . .
And there is naught to do but follow—lest
The hissing shadows prove my final plight.

VI. The Trail Between Two Trees

The witch-light leads me to a pair of trees,
Which frame a scene not seen to either side—
A haunting trail where goblins might abide,
Strange in the moon's soft silver sorceries,
Where blood-black leaves go swirling ever by,
And monstrous trees with wicked grins and wide
Wait the unwary with their claws, and wheeze
Amid the woodland's sad, eternal sigh.

I hesitantly set out on this trail
Of unknown perils, lest the witch-light fly.
The trees entwine behind me, barring me
From turning back; and in the autumn gale,
A phantom shaped of leaves and lunacy
Beckons to me, whose whispered words impale
My heart with sweetness and with misery.

The Trail Between Two Trees

VII. The Pumpkin King

There is a place the hissing shadows shun—
A lonely hill whereto they will not go,
Whose sloping sides are lurid with the glow
Of jack-o'-lanterns—nigh enough to stun
The eye accustomed to the dark of night.
Above the pumpkin-patch that sprawls below,
Enthroned upon its crest, a giant one
Wickedly grins down from its lofty height.

I make obeisance to the Pumpkin King,
Whose evil visage twists in cruel delight
With every bow I reverently make
Unto the mold, where worshipful I cling.
And when at last I stand up and betake
Me down the hillside darkly flickering,
The jack-o'-lanterns titter in my wake.

VIII. The Wood of Hissing Shadows

The road grows darker as the trees begin
To crowd in closer, like a living cage;
It seems that I have stepped into a page
Out of a haunting story. . . . Will I win
Through such a wood where shadow reigns supreme,
Whose vault of branches ever seems to wage
War with the stars, which seek some small way in
To glimpse the floor where grinning mushrooms teem . . . ?

The Pumpkin King

The shadows of my fears wax awfully
Amid this gloom unchallenged by the beam
Of moon or star, lit only by the light
Of lanterns hung but intermittently.
I pray the Pumpkin King has favored me . . .
For hissing shadows of essential night
Watch from behind the trees, just out of sight.

IX. The Cemetery of Dead Dreamers

Amid the mist, I spy a pointed fence
Covered in withered vines, whose Gothic gate
Swings in the wind—or has some wraith of late
Gone just before me? Filled with reverence,
I enter there the cemetery grounds
And visit graves of those who met their fate
Dreaming too far in haunted lands, and thence
Dreaming to death . . . beyond all mortal bounds.

Reflecting darkly on how such a doom
Could claim my brethren, suddenly the sounds
Of fallen leaves disturbed as by a dress
Dragging across them, and a sweet perfume,
Entice me through the mist. . . . What sorceress
Has led me to this solemn marble tomb
That bears my name, I dare not even guess.

X. The Muttering Mushroom

A croaking voice allures me to the verge
Of twilight woodland—low, as nigh the ground,
And difficult to hark, as if the sound
Comes from some tiny thing yet to emerge.
It leads me to a headstone that the trees
Have overtaken and stand ranked around
In timeless march, on which no longer dirge
Or epitaph illumes Time's mysteries.

I bend me down unto the very earth,
Seeking the source of such strange litanies—
And lo! a mushroom with a mouth relates
A buried dreamer's dreams with daemon mirth.
Its gibbered visions hint at what awaits
Unwary dreamers who would prove their worth
By entering through Nightmare's darkest gates.

XI. The Windows

Have I imagined everything?—Have I
But roamed the woods in mad delirium?
Was I so drunk with Night's aconitum
To chase chimeras whither they would fly?
For up ahead I spy the spectral glow
Of windows, weirdened by residuum
Of centuries of mist and rime, that vie
With arabesques of blackness forth to show.

I know these windows . . . for I oft have stared
Into Yorehaven's eyes, which seem to know
Uncounted secrets that I fain would learn,
But only strange reflections ever shared.
But maybe *she* would know . . . the raven-haired,
Seductive temptress curvèd like an urn,
Whose silhouette invites my blood to burn.

XII. The Shadow of Yorehaven

I stumble into town, but something seems
Not quite the same . . . the angles all are wrong;
Above the twisting streets, the gables throng
With crazy closeness, as if warped by dreams.
The houses stretch, contorting toward a moon
Whose gaze pursues me as I race along
The weirdly narrowed streets, its baleful beams
Burning with madness that must claim me soon.

So desperate to escape this hateful eye,
I rap upon a door, lest I should swoon—
It opens to reveal a revenant
With swirling eyes of witch-fire! And I fly
From the distorted face of one who went
Into the woods, whom we had thought to die—
Yorehaven's boldest absinthe-celebrant.

XIII. The Bookshop

I know this place . . . this shop of ancient books
Where must of rotting tomes enchants the air,
For it was here—or maybe it was there?—
That I would scour the gargoyle-guarded nooks
In search of crowning works of decadence,
Or necromancy—manuscripts so rare
That they are only found by him who looks
On evil shelves with ghoulish diligence.

Seeking the Crimson Tome, I step inside—
And *all* the books are crimson! I commence
To rummage madly through the mocking tomes,
Burning with rage that I should be denied!
But halting hopelessly, twin metronomes—
As of stilettos trotting just outside—
Make me again as one whom nightward roams.

XIV. Transformation

Arriving at the farther verge of town,
No longer do I fear the leering moon;
It howls within me, morbidly in tune
With my demeanor, which begins to drown
In murky depths of madness. How I smile
To see the trees that beckon me with brown
And withered limbs, while harking to the rune
Of a weird poem sung with woman's wile. . . .

Or do I merely hear the strangeful sigh
Of autumn wind that whispers through the trees?
I stand and listen to the night awhile,
And hear her haunting voice again . . . and hie
Into the forest, desperate to seize
Whatever temptress chants this lullaby
That fills my soul with midnight mysteries.

XV. A Mirror Image

The pathway takes me to a glade where stands
An ancient house—none other than my own;
There is the candle that all night has shone
To lead me home from dream-infested lands.
Yet why it lights the window on the left,
When in the *right* one's nightwind it had blown,
Presents a puzzle; maybe absent hands
Had placed it wrong, half-sleeping, sense-bereft.

Dismissing this, I glance up at the moon—
And realize its deathly face is cleft
By a black chimney which, when normal, rears
Up on the *right*. . . . Now evilly immune
To the illusion, my perception clears:
A mirror image?—yes. But which is hewn
Merely of mirror? Sureness disappears.

XVI. The Beckoning Hand

Standing before my darkly mirrored home,
I shrink before the jack-o'-lanterns' light—
I have become a vampire of the night,
Unable to abide aught but the gloom.
I struggle to regain humanity—
To rid my blood of midnight's aconite—
To cross the threshold barred to wraiths that roam
The eldritch ways of night eternally.

But just as I begin to back away
Into the woods whose shadows call to me,
The door begins to open . . . and a hand
Gloved in black velvet beckons me to stay.
It motions me to quit the shadowland
And come inside, with graceful, female sway . . .
And I cannot but heed its dark command.

XVII. Necromancy

The house is empty, in all ways the same
As I had left it, save in strange reverse;
There are my shelves of dark, exquisite verse,
And crumbling grimoires of nefandous fame.
I open one, and laugh to see the script
That I could never read now rendered tame;
I speak aloud a dark, exquisite curse,
Which claims to raise the dead up from the crypt.

A wizard wind awakens in the night,
Causing the candle on the ledge to flare,
As in a foul, mephitic wind up-whipped
From catacombs in nighted, charnel flight.
And out the window, wrought of moonlight rare,
A host of perished dreamers comes in sight,
Bearing to me the book that they would share.

XVIII. Initiation

By candlelight I read the Crimson Tome—
Here are the nightmares that I sought to find!
My senses totter, sight goes nearly blind,
To read what they who tasted midnight's pome
Inscribed in crimson ink of what they dreamed—
Of what mad prodigies they glimpsed behind
The ebon curtain of the midnight gloam,
Before their broken minds in madness screamed.

And at the end I find some virgin leaves,
Saved just for me by those who went before,
Whereon I scrawl the nightmares that have teemed
Upon my sight, whose shadow ever cleaves.
While all around me, grave and deathly hoar,
There stand the dreamers I have read of eves
When open windows yawn on night's dark shore.

XIX. The Black Kiss

I feel a strange sensation on my cheek
Like phantom lips in passion pressed thereon;
The mirror proves my visage weirdly wan—
But far more troubling, causing me to shriek:
The ebon kiss-mark branded on my face,
Sprouting fine tendrils as of hebenon
Blossoming blackly through my blood to seek
My thirsty heart, which strange lust makes to race.

I smash this monstrous image, and I flee
Into the forest, keeping fiendish pace;
For I am followed by the eidolon
Of a pale woman draped seductively
In a long gown black as oblivion,
Whose gorgeous figure starts from every tree,
Alike the fatal nymph who hunts the faun.

XX. Dream Decay

I am more dream than man . . . my body fades
Into the shadows, lost forevermore.
Traveled too long have I beyond the door
To darkest dreams, amid this land of shades.
Now I am doomed forever to remain,
As one who proves the sleep of mandragore,
To roam with phantoms through forgotten glades
Where a dead moon holds mad, eternal reign.

The Black Kiss

All memories of home grow dim and far,
Like dreams that in the morning sadly drain
Down gulfs forgotten. Yet the growing gloom
Of human thought is litten by the star
Of a lone candle bright as Achernar,
Whereto I will return to tell my doom
Ere I depart into the midnight brume.

UNPLEASANT DREAMS

Nocturnal Poet

Leave me alone. The visions I would glimpse
    All scatter at intrusion of late-calling souls—
Scatter into the shadows like the imps
    That watch this candle-flame with eyes like wicked coals.

Leave me in silence—say no other word.
    For hearken I to voices hid from normal ears—
Strange, subtle voices that few men have heard,
    That sigh in crimson drapes through which the full moon leers.

Hark midnight's chime—go—close my chamber door.
    For open lies a blank leaf in this crimson tome—
This tome wherein I now shall scribe the lore
    My daemon muse imparts beneath the night's black dome.

O daemon muse! what have you dreamed of nights
    When tapers falter in a ghost-awoken wind?
What succubi have bared their pale delights
    Unto your lusting gaze—tell me, how have you sinned?

What secrets have you wrested from the crypt—
    What wisdom have you pried from cold lips of the dead?
What purple poisons from gold goblets sipped—
    And whither, drunken with such draughts, durst you to tread?

What artful sorceresses have you sought
    In moonlit gardens where vampiric roses grow?
What necromancies at your robes have caught
    As you have traveled those dim ways that dreamers know?

Tell me of eldritch things, O daemon muse,
    My raven quill rests on this parchment patiently;
This haunted hour of dreams, do not refuse
    To me the strange, nocturnal visions destined me.

The Crimson Tome

Open no more the Crimson Tome—
Its pages teem
With demon moans in haunted gloam
Of eldritch dream.

Read not the verses writ therein
In crimson ink,
Lest spells weighed down with death begin
Your soul to sink.

The Chimeras of Midnight

The reassurance of the sun is fled,
    And midnight's dark chimeras take its place—
    A plane of nightmare, vast and void as space,
Unfurls horizons dark and fraught with dread.

Which way I turn, I face the gloating stare
    Of fiend or phantom starting from the dark,
    Dimly illumed in crimson, and I hark
To screams that comet through the silent air.

All evil thoughts embarred by sunlight's beams
    Escape their cells at this unhallowed hour,
    And with a warped and disproportioned power,
Inflate to monstrous size and crowd my dreams.

Unpleasant Dreams

One night I closed my eyes to court a dream,
And though the taper bravely fought to stay
The close and crowding darkness, keep at bay
Those cacodaemons that at midnight scheme,
A more terrific night eclipsed my eyes—
An inner night from which remembrance shies.

Half-formless horrors spawned from primal fear
Swam through a murk of nightmare infinite—
Adown the blackest labyrinths filled with fright,
I fled from phantoms drawing ever near.
And though I struggled, dread entanglement
In midnight alleys was my punishment.

Long scaly talons snatched and tore my shirt,
And evil faces my mad flight observed;
And as down twisting ways I dodged and swerved,
A ghoulish laughter worked to wreak more hurt
On a morale defeated to its dregs—
Only a mindless panic moved my legs.

Dangerous gateways dreamers' eyelids are.
Small wonder Nature shuts our eyes on sleep!
If had my dreaming gaze not glimpsed so deep!
If had but shone some more forgiving star!
Then might the pleasantness of dream be spared.
It has been too long since to dream I dared.

Halloween

Grim pumpkin faces mock the dark
    With blazing goblin grins:
Each flickeringly brands its mark
On blackened air, mysteriarch
        Of bale that soon begins . . .
Of weird diablerie that reigns till dawn its throne rewins.

The crimson leaves of autumn flee
        A coming nameless dread:
They swirl through lamplight witchery,
And crawl across the shadowed lea
        Where no one dares to tread,
For fear of devils in the fog, and being faerie-led.

All doors and shutters fast are locked,
        The children run and hide.
As midnight time is ticked and tocked,
Their parents peer through cracks unblocked
        With fearful eyes and wide,
At dreadful shapes and things with wings that through the
    shadows glide.

An ill wind slithers in the trees,
        Which glowing eyes conceal;
A lantern dances in the breeze,

Illuming hints of blasphemies
　　　　Best never to reveal . . .
Weird shapes that waver by and leave a wake of the Unreal.

Pale corpse-lights flicker in the air
　　　　Like embers blown from hell.
Those souls that spy their ghostly flare
Remember stories, and beware
　　　　Of what the legends tell. . . .
They hasten on their way, imperiled by an olden spell.

A sluggish fog engulfs the street
　　　　Like smoke from cauldrons vile:
Within it phantom faces fleet,
But floating forth, they oft retreat—
　　　　Before a crueler smile!
Those houses without jack-o'-lanterns face a spectral trial.

The elves are sneaking over the sward,
　　　　Invisible—but *heard;*
For on this eve the faerie horde
Awakes over this night to lord,
　　　　Whose normal bourns are blurred. . . .
They curse the scarecrow-guarded crops, and cause the milk
　　to curd.

An owlet's hoot bestirs the fog,
　　　　So haunting, desolate;
Somewhere anear the final frog
Quiets its croaks within the bog

Whence came weird sounds of late. . . .
But when deep Silence settles in, *true* terror lies in wait.

Behind the rusty, Gothic spears
        That fence the graveyard round,
White tapers tipped with fiery tears
Call back the dead of former years
        From death's abyss profound:
Amid the mausoleums roaming, restless dead abound.

Grim gargoyles guard the steeple tall,
        Wherein is housed the bell;
But in the moonlight's silver thrall,
And autumn dark's phantasmal pall—
        When booms the midnight knell—
Those sentinels of sanctity become the fiends of hell!

The moon is seen through filmy clouds,
        A skull in moldy soil;
Above the tower, swarming crowds
Of wraiths display their trailing shrouds
        Athwart a silver foil;
Whilst on the ground the minions of the moon begin to moil.

Above the distant hinterland,
        Whose trees dark secrets screen,
There hangs a faint, arcane command—
A pagan deity seems to stand
        Above a blaze pale green. . . .
Old incantations, ancient spells, return on Halloween.

Mandrake

Thinking to make a philter from its root,
I plucked a mandrake from the haunted fen—
A shriek to crack the very crystal stars
Tore through the evil and oppressive air.

The torn up mandrake's pain was absolute—
Yet mine was greater, *more* my torment then!
Beneath the red and evil eye of Mars,
I beat the tuber till no life was there.

Divers alchemic apparatus worked
To yield a drop of star-urged potency;
Toasting to Death, Forgetfulness, and Sleep,
I tipped the black drop to my eager lips.

It was a poison in whose Lethe lurked
The echoes of the mandrake's misery,
Lending a direness sure to make it seep
More quickly in, to soak death's dormant pips.

A deeper darkness pressed upon my eyes—
A silence fell of a completer Night—
But still the specter of the world remained,
And madness mated with my blind despair!

And through my darkness echoed mandrake cries,
More piercing for my lone, enlimboed plight.
I knew it then: the magick moon had waned—
The evil marsh-mist had bewitched the air.

The Fatal Flower

The fatal flower out of nowhere came—
A single huge, strange blossom in the mead:
The villagers agreed
It bore resemblance to the nightshade bloom—
A primal nightmare version of the same—
A horrid relict from some steaming epoch without name—
An ornament of doom.

Around that purple despot of disease,
Beneath a fog of perfume poisonous,
As if a succubus
Had breathed upon it, a gray ring of grass
Grew outward from the stem. The birds and bees
That had explored the plant their need for nectar to appease
Lay still and dead, alas.

The circle of decay that outward crept
Killed all it touched—the trees grew sere and brown,
Their shriveled fruits fell down:
Plums, apples, peaches, pomes of every kind,
Lay rotting on the sward where corpses slept.
Yet, strange to say, no swarms of flies athwart that banquet
    swept—
None but the Worm there dined.

At last the gray plague reached the village verge,

But none among them could defeat the flower—

All those who braved its bower

Fell prey to fatal languor, not to wake.

A deathly silence was the only dirge

When all lay still in coiling lilac fog like some huge gurge

Upon a poison lake.

Soul Rot

There is a fungus fruiting in my soul—
A solitary toadstool rooted fast
With mats of tendrils that my life-force leech,
Causing a rot that nothing can control.

Slowly it spreads its poison parasol,
And ever higher does it inch its reach
Up from the bottom of my soul, to cast
A spreading shade, upon my soul a pall.

Amid the dark of its eclipsing cap,
Which showers spores with rank fecundity,
Sprout tiny mushrooms thriving on the rot—
Dead happiness become corruption-heap.

Be not surprised if sprouts upon my tomb
A bloated toadstool. My sick soul will not
Escape my corpse, for it will hopelessly
Be wrapped in fungal threads of mummied doom.

The Darkness Within

Trapped in the deepest dungeon of my soul,
    Abides an oozing, black, amorphous blob,
Which strains against its chains—its blind, mad goal:
    To enter my heart's throb.

Homunculi that heed my conscience spear
    It with subduing tridents, but the beast
In ebon slime absorbs them when they near,
    And bloats on its foul feast.

Increased in strength, unstayed by piercing prongs,
    It viscously escapes its iron gyves,
And slinks off to commit dark sins and wrongs,
    Spurred on by evil drives.

And so the darkness in me wins the day;
    Its creeping poison courses through my heart.
Enthralled by darkness, I must now obey
    All that my imps impart.

What the Moon Saw

I saw the moon lift up in fear a face,
    To stare in terror at the vesper vault above;
    It seemed to see some monstrous thing whereof
I could discern in starless azure not a trace.

Climbing so high athwart the welkin's wall,
    I think it spied a dark truth hidden from my ken—
    A stellar secret, sky-concealed from men,
Of which the mute stars hint to those in their strange thrall.

The Treachery of the Stars

Behind the sky's blank blue stirs treachery:
    Unseen, the stars array the dooms of men
    Athwart the darkling waste beyond day's ken,
In argent runes of astral sorcery.

Like diamond dice cast out across the night
    By stellar demons, not quite come to rest,
    The stars prepare, upon the palimpsest
Of former fortunes, Signs of dreadful might.

Malefic moons and wrathful suns align
    To lend their malice to the monstrous scheme;
    And planets, prisoned in their orbits, dream
Of wreaking chaos and their bales combine.

Upon the placid azure dome of day,
    In fleecy cloud are written fairytales
    Of future's promise. . . . But that fancy veils
A flaming death that streaks from far away.

Sirius

I felt the icy lances of its rays
Before I even dared to lift my gaze
    Up to the purpling sky—
For Sirius had risen from the haze,
     Frore winter's eye.

It was a phare of sapphire in the night,
Irradiant with strange, unearthly light
    That whined within my mind—
Even when I had turned my stricken sight
     Relief to find!

I fled in terror down that country lane,
Sheltering from the star's unblinking bane
    Behind a titan tree—
But *still* I felt its gaze, without refrain!—
     I could but flee!

The stellar torture every step increased—
The howling winter wind not in the least
    Could mask the astral scream
That pierced my pulsing mind from out the east,
     Deep as a dream!

Sirius

At last I faltered on a barren hill,
Alone beneath the sky with broken will,
    And I could not but bow
Before the Dog-Star. . . . Whereupon no ill
    Disturbed my brow.

And They Took Her Away

By the moon's silver light I held tryst with my love
On a cursed, ruined castle the village above;
O how sweet were the lips of my darling, my dove—
    Ere they took her away.

O the stars they were hinting of terrible things!
But my love did not know of what Betelgeuse brings . . .
So I troubled her not over faint, flapping wings—
    And they took her away.

O her face it was fair as the Vesperal Star!
And her long, golden locks were as moon-shimmers are!
But her eyes, they gazed strangely, as if from afar—
    Ere they took her away.

And they tore her, they bore her, from out my embrace—
Did those green, wingèd demons from black pits of space!
And they flew with my love toward the moon's laughing face—
    And they took her away.

Corpse Moon

Dead rotting hands reach from the cemetery mold,
    Like ghastly weeds that writhe in ghostly, stagnant mist,
    To hail a monstrous, skull-like moon that keeps its tryst
With midnight, raising tides of corpses long grown cold.

The Crimson Unicorn

Foredoomed is he who meets that mare—
    The crimson unicorn!
Glimpse red within her woodland lair
    And one nears danger's bourn.

They say she gets her sanguine hue
    By bathing in the blood
Of humans she has skewered through
    For ravaging her wood.

But warning always does she send—
    The charnel drone of flies
That always as a cloud attend
    The blood that on her dries.

Who hears the swarm, or breathes the blast
    Of stench that soon entails,
Must try to quit the wood in haste,
    Its verdant gyves and gaols.

But if the trees care not to let
    Flee who offends their guard,
With snares of vines the wood will net
    Him and his flight retard.

And then the crimson unicorn
    Will leap from out the leaves,
And fiercely pierce with her black horn
    His chest while yet it heaves.

The Thirst of Count Aster

So weak was I with wanting, weak for want of blood
    To sate my ancient thirst, my terrible, ancient thirst,
That soon my thoughts grew darker than the glooms that brood
    Within this castle of the damned and the accursed. . . .

So weak was I that scarcely could I even stir,
    Nor could I leave my throne, my throne of misery—
So weak that I would have to wait for her—for her
    Whose presence alone dispelled my deathless agony.

Ah God, if there can be a God, your angel strayed
    Into a den of evil worse than any hell!
Your fairest, purest maiden, trusting, unafraid,
    Entered the shadows of my court by sunset's knell.

The ponderous doors were parted, showing purpling skies,
    And through the narrow crack there came the fairest fair;
Her lantern was a fallen star unto my eyes,
    And echoes of her stepping stirred the stagnant air.

"Count Aster, I have come as I have always come
    To sit with you awhile, to ease your loneliness;
How well I know the curse to which you now succumb—
    Yet where all would forsake, I offer a friend's caress.

"How ashen are you grown, the visage of the grave
    Has warped your proud and handsome face so terribly—
Yet still a kindness clings to you, and I would save
    What goodness clings unto your soul so desperately."

"Come close, my child, that I may kiss your beautiful brow—
    No fairer creature ever walked this cruel earth.
How dear, how dear you are to me, and dearer now
    That nevermore will I behold your youth and mirth. . . ."

And saying so, I sprang to clutch her pulsing neck—
    But she was faster! and I fell unto the floor.
I begged forgiveness, howled her name, a broken wreck—
    But she was gone, forever gone, forevermore!

Of all the burdens buried in my ancient heart,
    Her screams refuse to rest—their torment echoes still
Throughout my nighted soul, my soul nigh torn apart
    By her eternal absence nothing now can fill.

Ah, curse the day this wretched curse left me bereft
    Of her that was my only joy, my only light!
Now pain and loneliness are all that I have left—
    These, and the quiet solace of eternal night.

Better that I had quelled my diabolic thirst
    With blood of murderers and thieves, but I abstained,
Till at the last, when hunger grew its very worst,
    I betrayed her trust—oh God, I would I had refrained!

For every drop of blood within her holy veins,

    I will weep ten thousand tears in woe and penitence;

And when at last the fount of grief has ceased its rains,

    My sword shall pierce my heart—a paltry recompense.

A Vampire Fear

A vampire fear stalks the darkening twilight—
　　The Undead draw near in each shadowy copse;
The fiery red sun, like some faltering stylite,
　　To fall has begun behind black mountaintops.

A castle perched high in Carpathian mountains
　　Against the dark sky looms like some evil peak;
The wolves are all howling, and mortals are fountains
　　Of life for the prowling vampires to seek.

Blue witch-fires burn in dark caverns of forest
　　As villagers yearn for the far morning light;
They hang garlic cloves from the eaves—for their sorest
　　Of fears is what roves through the mist-haunted night.

All hands clasp in prayer or clutch stakes for destroying
　　Those monsters that bear no remorse for the blood
They've sucked from the necks of pale maidens, while toying
　　With all that bedecks their full-blossomed maidhood.

A flapping black stream erupts from a ruined tower,
　　And like a bad dream, the bats sweep past the moon,
On which—as the bell strikes a forsaken hour—
　　Appears a dark spell of vampirical boon.

The Scarlet Font

Meet me beside the font whose cherubim,
    Expressing sculptured pain, pour ruby blood
    From moaning mouths to feed a burning flood,
Where nenuphars night-black, nocturnal, swim,
And waft a philtered breath so deathly dim.

Come listen to the scarlet purl and splash,
    Wherein reveals the faerie of the font
    Half-spoken secrets that red demons chaunt;
And bow your pallid face, drop each dark lash,
To scry in scarlet depths delights so rash. . . .

See how the argent shards of lunar light
    Sparkle upon the gules sanguinolent!
    See how the stars that gem night's firmament
Stare down at rosy rubies from their height—
For us exalted treasures here alight!

Observe the toads that bathe in carnal wine,
    And how the bats all light to sate their thirst;
    O vampiress, observe that you are cursed,
And soon must drink deep of the bloody brine. . . .
Quaff of the font, then press your lips to mine.

Vampiric Roses

Vampiric roses verge a sanguine pool,
Drooping empetalled mouths to drink thereof,
Whilst reeking mist of scarlet stales above
Their awful quaffing, shunned by hag and ghoul.

Such roses' thirst might stand for long-craved love—
The drunken suck of lovers, crazed and cruel,
At Passion's philter, till its fire should cool
In scarlet swoon, flushed limbs fast interwove.

Blood

Give me your blood that beats so hot within,
    Like crimson wine conflagrant with desire!
I hear its coursing din
    Like cataracts of raging, vital fire!

Your pallid body, passively supine
    Upon a velvet divan deathly black,
Is like an ivory scrine
    For scarlet pleasures that unchain life's rack. . . .

Your sable mane allures with its perfume—
    Your ruby lips are parted, breathing spells—
Your blue eyes star the gloom—
    But blood alone my hell-deep craving quells!

Your alabastrine throat, your choicest curve,
    Is the sole chalice wherefrom I would drain
The wine that you would serve—
    Your pulsing life straight from your fervid vein!

Give me your blood that thunders through you now,
    Volcanic lava striving for release
From under trembling snow,
    And drift into a dim and opiate peace.

Bathory

I will fill this gold bathtub to brimming
  With the blood of uncountable girls;
I will soak in it, utterly swimming,
  Wearing only my jewels and pearls!

I will soak it all through my dark tresses,
  I will smear it across my white breasts!
I will drink it from finest of glasses—
  Vintages of my loveliest guests!

I will lure fair young girls to my castle—
  Lovely virgins alone will suffice;
I will make every maiden my vassal
  In my palace of pleasure and vice!

I will suck each sweet mouth of its kisses—
  I will taste every blasphemous fruit!
I will plumb all of Pleasure's abysses!—
  Till I lust for a different pursuit. . . .

One by one all my servants will vanish
  To the music of echoing screams.
Pretty corpses will serve to replenish
  My gold tub of immortal red dreams.

Bathory

The Crimson Tome

Bathed in blood, I shall live on forever
    With a beauty that never shall fade!—
Countess Erzsebet Bathory never
    Shall be rivaled by empress or maid.

Siren of the Dead

Waiting beneath an ancient, rotted tree
Fixed with a cross that marks forebodingly
    The Forest of the Dead,
Her icy eyes are phares that lure the flames
Of travelers gone mad with amour's aims,
    Who seek her sordid bed.

She gestures with a finger, worm-like, gray,
That burrows through the hearts of those who stray
    Too near to where she rests.
Her purple lips pour forth sweet promises,
Expelling spiders with each word she says,
    Which crawl adown her breasts.

Like moths that dare the burning doom of fire,
Men prove amid her pale limbs dark desire,
    A soulless, pulseless love.
And when she parts her draping, raven hair
To kiss her victims, wisps of inky air
    Breathe forth, of Slumber wove.

Her lovers numberless grow limp and pale,
Locked to a kiss that kills, till their hearts fail,
    Lifeless against her own.

Yet still they rise, as puppets of her plague,
To wander dumbly through a woodland vague
    With fog, where Death holds throne.

Beneath black boughs that arabesque a sky
Of weary gray, they wander through the dry
    Dead leaves of vanished years.
And nevermore will they know lust for her,
Whose long dead limbs dark magick keeps astir
    To tempt whoever nears.

My Darling Bride

You look so gorgeous in your lacy gown,
My darling bride! Your perfect, pallid face
Glows like a witch-light in this spectral place
Of crumbling tombs and trees that darkly frown.
Let all the specters of the dead attend—
Goblins and ghouls our wedding-vows shall grace!
And for our priest, a corpse of withered brown
Its rotting sanctity shall kindly lend!

In life your answer tore my heart . . . but now
You give me full devotion without end.
And though your soul now follows Charon's prow,
And though a coldness clings unto your brow,
You now are mine. Long have I dreamed of this—
To steal from you one sweetly rancid kiss. . . .
Beneath this moon, my bride, we shall know bliss.

NOCTURNAL LOVERS
PART I

Succubus

The tapers burn with passion strange,
And warm the midnight gloom;
The darkness undergoes a change—
An amaranthine mist
Appears with sweet perfume.

Divaned upon a violet cloud
Of sensuous, warm dream,
The demon, like a nymph endowed,
Descends . . . and I am kissed
By lips that purr my name.

Her lust-conflagrant love is cold,
Her bosom harbors chill
Of Dis' deepest ice—her hold
Grows frore with fiercest passion,
As buried bodies will.

I gaze in her infernal eyes
And spy the burning Damned
Who've lain with her, and mingled sighs
With her in lovers' fashion—
And let my soul be claimed.

Nocturnal Lover

Steal in through my window,
My moon-litten window,
From fall mists avernal,
My lover nocturnal.

I spy your pale figure,
Your dark-haired, horned figure,
With red eyes infernal,
My lover nocturnal.

O demon, hie hither,
Through dark woodland, hither,
From night sempiternal,
My lover nocturnal.

Enwrap me with pleasures,
Your hot, hellish pleasures—
My limbs lie hibernal,
My lover nocturnal.

Corrupt me with kisses,
Your soul-drinking kisses—
O grant life eternal,
My lover nocturnal.

Dark Poetry

Sing me the blackest spells
Composed in scarlet hells,
My demon mistress, spare no magick word.
Open your crimson book,
Wherein no man may look,
And read the runes whose witchcraft can't be cured.

The serpent's deadly hiss
Your sweet tongue turns to bliss,
Each syllable entwining my dark heart.
I'm drunken with the dance
Of teeth and tongue, a trance
Comes over me, seduced by your dark art.

With each seductive verse
I'm made a slave, or worse;
You know it well—that smirk, that lingering glance. . . .
My burning soul is yours,
My hunger for you roars,
Your poetry is poisoned with romance.

Witch's Charms

A charming witch's smile
  Enthralls with force of all her spells—
  More dire than poison asphodels,
A charming witch's smile.

A gorgeous witch's gaze
  Is like a twain of flaming runes—
  Makes rise the blood like tidal moons,
A gorgeous witch's gaze.

A lovely witch's voice
  Is like the chalice pouring wine—
  An incantation soft, malign,
A lovely witch's voice.

A sultry witch's scent
  Is steaming wafture of the rose—
  Savors of some Circean close,
A sultry witch's scent.

A tempting witch's touch
  Entrances like a snake's caress—
  Enslaves with slow seductiveness,
A tempting witch's touch.

A lustful witch's kiss
    Is hot with passion of the Pit—
    Pours forth a poison cucurbit,
A lustful witch's kiss.

A Heart Defiled

Your poison arrow pierced my naked heart,
    Spreading warm venom through my fevered veins.
You shot it surely, with seductive art—
With a mere flick of eyelash fired a dart
    In pyrrhic pleasures dipped, and precious pains.

Now I can think of only you, my love—
    Eyes that enslaved me, lips that subtly smiled—
For I am damned by angels high above
To feed upon your charms, a vampire of
    Perfume and flesh, to fill a heart defiled.

O Pale Temptress

O pale temptress so fair,
You of dark, dwale-crowned hair,
Who dwells in the old tower
Dark trees strain to hide,
If for one more drugged hour
You'd lie by my side
On your deep, violet divan . . .
My last could be sighed.

O pale temptress divine,
Whose mauve eyes once held mine,
Will no philter avail
Your lips to regain?—
Since my life soon will fail,
For poison I'm fain. . . .
For your kiss be forgiven—
Though by it I'm slain.

Ashiel

No sorceress has ever cast
    A stronger spell
Than that placed on me three moons past
    By Ashiel.

In misty moonlit garths where grows
    The asphodel
Of poison purple, and the rose
    As red as hell,

She worked her witch's charms on me,
    Worked them so well;
Bedrugged by perfume, sleepily,
    For her I fell.

In her bewitching gray-blue eyes,
    As down a well,
I seemed to sink through starry skies,
    Vaguely unwell.

We loved upon an ivy couch—
    I could not tell
If truly did a skull I touch,
    From me an ell.

84

But when she pressed her lips to mine,
    So full and fell—
A crimson orchid sweet as wine
    Or hydromel—

And when I drowned amid her hair
    Of caramel,
And felt her pallid breasts and bare,
    With lust a-swell,

The monstrous specters of my fears
    She did dispel,
And all my weariness of years
    She soon did quell.

My withered heart now beats its last
    Sepulchral knell.
Three moons agone I held her fast—
    Fair Ashiel!

Ashiel

Ashiel's Gem

Nestled between the lifted breasts of Ashiel,
Hung on a fine gold chain that lazily cascades
Adown her milky curves, a gem of crimson shades,
So dazzling in the candlelight, the languid swell
And fall of her breath rides—a cold, exquisite hell.

Within that ruby oubliette are trapped the souls
Of lovers past that failed to sate her dark desires.
Therein they must abide as long as she requires—
Through centuries of crimson gloom and haunting doles
More deep than mortal ones, in chill of ultimate poles.

With absent fingers toying with her gem, she stares
With listless gray-blue eyes into the smoky gloom,
Made sweet with incense, of her lavish sleeping-room,
With parted scarlet lips that hope that unawares
Will they be caught by phantom kisses from dead years.

The gem makes cold the bosom countless silk simars
Were torn apart to bare . . . her tresses warm them not;
For cold and cruel, the doom of those in that gem caught.
For them the sorceress' candles are as stars
That weakly shine through crimson skies and ruby bars.

Ashiel's Mirror

Combing her long and darkly lustrous mane,
With languor-laden eyelids, Ashiel
Admires her image in a mirror made
In semblance of a yawning demon's head:

Her sinful flesh is fair as porcelain;
Her purple lids crown lapis eyes that dwell
Upon her own; her lips that lately prayed
To fiends infernal burn a bloody red.

Her beauty would befit a Grecian fane,
Yet gazing in her glass, she cannot quell
A terrible lust for beauty not displayed
By any goddess yet alive or dead.

Her perfect features, fair beyond all gain,
She fain would make more fair—and yet no spell,
No sorcery avails—none have arrayed
Her with more charms, how darkly she has pled.

So she grows bored of all things in this vein—
She tires of beauty! How to end this hell
Of unimproved perfection unallayed?—
Something from which all beauty has been bled. . . .

Now mirrored sits a corpse, reflected plain—
A rotted lover from a dungeon-cell:
The mirror's boredom strangely seems to fade . . .
Its yawn a smile, its newfound craving fed.

Ashiel's Prisoner

So many moons I spent pinned down beneath
         Her breasts,
Shackled to crimson sheets and drunk with meath,
   A helpless slave to her perverse behests.

Her lustful thighs a vice were unto mine,
         Her lips
Panted hot pleasures from their scarlet scrine,
   And demon moans of passionate eclipse.

In cataracts of raven wildly fell
         Her hair,
Down ivory curves kissed as with fires of hell,
   Shining in torchlight, squirming, burning, bare.

Without the window's arch, the stars scarce matched
         Her eyes
In icy shine—through half-closed lids they watched
   With languid lust her prisoner, her prize.

And after hours of fire I lay within
         Her arms,
In mockery of romance, scorched with sin,
   Trapped by the bedpost-teraphims' dark charms.

Then I was left with but the ghost of her
        Perfume,
And petals plucked from nightshade—to endure,
    Till Ashiel again would grace my gloom.

Ashiel's Diary

With sunset sparkling in her sapphire eyes,
    And sighs perfumed with rhyme upon red lips,
    And sable mane wild in a wind that whips
In purple drapes that give on vesper skies,

Beside the tower window, Ashiel
    Inscribes a purple tome with poetry—
    A book of magick, romance, blasphemy,
Whose silver clasp but opens for a spell.

But when the moon drifts nigh on night's dark shore,
    She shuts the Diary of a Sorceress,
    And like a proud, bacchantic paganess,
She drops her purple robes upon the floor.

Her lover-slave, though shackled to the wall,
    Reaches as if to touch her flaunted flesh—
    But Ashiel, desiring something fresh,
Pursues her Muse instead, her fancy's call.

She bathes her body in the moon's white beams,
    Baring her breasts unto the starry vast,
    So that a spark of starfire might be passed
Into her soul, to flame when next she dreams.

And all the while there rests her purple tome
    Upon her escritoire, to wait her pen,
    Till by the twilight's violet skies, again
Will she record the whispers of the gloam.

Ashiel's Ritual

Vesperal mists of purple creep upon
Surrounding mountain peaks as Ashiel
Prepares a hilltop spell at Samhain's dawn—
The scarlet sunset of a year now gone.
Clad in a lacy, black and clinging dress,
Which never quite shows flesh enough to quell
Her captive's gaze...the gorgeous sorceress
Stands in the ghostly, clawing wind's caress.

Tracing with sapphire eyes her cryptic seal,
She sets its quarters with black asphodel,
Mandrake, witch-wine, and blood to make a deal
With demon lords that come a soul to steal. . . .
And pressing red lips to her prisoner's
One final time, she sighs as he endures
An awful fate that should have long been hers.

Three Poems After *Venus in Furs*

(The following three poems were inspired by *Venus in Furs*, by Leopold von Sacher-Masoch, translated by F. Savage, 1921)

Severin's Venus

There is a carven Venus in the park,
Whom I adore and worship—mostly when
The moonlight paints her marble blue, for then
She seems alive...a Goddess in the dark,
Bathing in moonbeams, proud and beautiful,
Yet cold and cruel . . . Mistress of all men
Who love her all the more so for her stark
White countenance, all prostrate, worshipful.

Stooping to kiss her queenly, cold white feet,
I press my head against the pedestal
On which she stands, in pagan prayer, replete
With slavish love for Venus, venom-sweet!
She loves me with a cold, indifferent heart,
And mocking smile, the triumph of all art—
O Venus, we can never be apart!

Wanda von Dunajew

She is my Venus rendered flesh . . . her hair
Falls in red tresses tameless as a fire!
Her eyes are demon emeralds of desire!
Her lips, the apple scheming Eve would share.
Draping her naked shoulders, sable fur
Flows head to foot, a cruel queen's attire,
Which, as she sprawls upon on her crimson chair,
Might bare her marble bust if she should stir.

The whip she plays with, held in her right hand,
Whose singing sting I often must endure,
The scepter is of her despotic rule,
Against which I, her slave, can never stand.
Bowing before her, I am but the stool
On which her resting feet, or kicks, will land,
According to her whim—now cold, now cruel.

Venus in Furs

(Adapted from the stanza given by Severin)

O place your foot upon your slave,
O Venus, demon of my dreams!
Among the shadows, dark and grave,
Your lounging body softly gleams.

O whip me as it pleases you,
O cruel and despotic queen!
Your sable fur and mien imbue
With monarch chill your eyes of green.

Make me your slave forevermore,
O Mistress—my Divinity!
Your flaming pagan tresses pour
Down marble breasts so terribly!

Be cruel to me, be cold and proud,
O Wanda, Venus wrapped in furs!
Your slave is favored if allowed
That mocking, crimson mouth of yours.

Note: The first stanza represents a slight alteration of that given in the novel. Line 3 appears verbatim; the others were slightly modified, to improve them poetically. The three stanzas that follow the first are entirely original.

Mistress of Torture

With sharply echoed steps, my Mistress comes
Into the dungeon, down the granite stairs;
Beneath a fanged grotesque that darkly stares,
The archway frames her figure—fear succumbs
To torrid lust for corset-tightened curves
Of black and crimson, like the spider wears;
She sports a scarlet smirk that somehow sums
Up appetite for passion's dark hors d'oeuvres. . . .

Her whip is Law, the pain provoked thereby,
An offering to devils that she serves—
The monstrous imps of Boredom, Madness, Lust,
Upon whose darkling altar I will die.
But though my body crumble down to dust,
In cold embrace of chains at last to lie—
The chains that bind my heart shall never rust.

Mistress of Torture

Priestess of Pleasure

O pagan priestess from an ancient frieze,
Presiding over Pleasure's mysteries,
Proffer your cup of gold with rubies set,
That I may drain its dark wine, and abet
The flow of Passion through enfevered veins,
Binding our bodies with the scarlet chains
Of lust unfettered. . . . No more wild a flow
Is to be found, save in your mane aglow
With light of torches out-flamed by your lips,
And by the burning in your moon-pale hips.
Give me your limbs as sensuously white
As sun-warm lilies in the languid light
Of sultry evenings, and enfold me there,
As in a land where naught of pain or care
Troubles the balmy breeze that is your breath.
Within that vale narcotic nigh as death,
Your rose-encrownèd brow shall be my moon,
Shining forever in nocturnal noon;
And your blue eyes shall serve as heaven's stars,
Brighter than all of girdled Algebar's,
Twinkling between the fulsome, soft, white hills
Of your uplifted breasts that passion fills,
Whose hilltop altars I will worship on
With purple kisses till the rosy dawn.
How I will delve into the fragrant gloom

Between those altars, where a rich perfume
As of long-perished flowers lingers still,
And drink thereof, profoundly drunk, until,
Wandering drowsily upward a stream
Of spice-immingled breath warm as a dream,
I will discover your lips' cup, and drink
A deeper stupor from their ruby brink.

The Demon and the Vampiress

I was a demon hot with such a lust
    As icy moonlight could not cool.
I smelled perfume of victims on each gust
    Of howling nightwind cold and cruel.

But mortal maidens never sated me,
    And forest nymphs but fanned my fire,
And succubi indulged but dreamily—
    It seemed that none shared my desire.

But as I haunted the autumnal glade,
    Lamenting to the stars my plight,
A vampiress appeared to me, and bade
    Me follow her into the night.

How sweet the fiend I followed through the mist!
    How bloody red her wicked lips!
How milky white her flesh no sun had kissed!
    How black the hair that passed her hips!

She led me to a castle on a hill,
    She took me up the twisting stair;
She dragged me down a torch-lit hallway, till
    We came at last into her lair.

It was a gloomy chamber, decadent
    With crimson rugs and tapestries;
Red candles gleamed on grim devices meant
    To mete out torture by degrees.

She shackled me with relish to the rack—
    I half bethought me to resist,
But ordinary romance seemed to lack
    The dark excitement of this tryst.

I studied her, her breasts so bountiful,
    Her every curve enfevered me;
She was voluptuously beautiful,
    A dark-eyed queen of blasphemy.

She flagellated me, and from each gash
    She licked the warmly welling blood;
She watched me with those dark eyes long of lash
    As she lapped up my scarlet flood.

And then she pressed her burning flesh to mine
    To brand me with a bloody kiss,
Then sank her fangs into my neck to dine
    Upon my blood in utter bliss.

And then it seemed my lust was drained from me,
    And in the sable eyes that gazed
Into my own, there welled a crimson sea
    Of lust that Lilit might have praised. . . .

She ravaged me with vigor terrible,
  She made me love-slave of her bower,
Her appetites beyond unbearable,
  Her moans resounding from her tower.

NOCTURNAL LOVERS
PART II

Dark Star of My Desire

For A. D.

Dark star of my desire,
You burn like crimson fire
In blackest caverns of my heart,
Where lurk ghoul and vampire.

You light those haunted ways,
The starless nights, dim days,
Where wander I, ever apart,
A wraith in twilight haze.

Dark Poetess of My Heart

For A. D.

Alone, by night, I scrawl my Gothic verse,
Yet solitude and darkness are my curse.
This candle-flame can't kindle my cold heart,
And phantoms of its light all from me part.
Yet in the haunted chambers of my mind,
The visage of a Goddess do I find—
That of a lovely witch with moon-blue eyes,
And flowing tresses dark as starless skies.

The poetry she whispers casts a spell
That breaks the chains that hold my heart in hell.
She banishes my demons of despair
With but a glance from her arresting stare.
If she could grant me but one scarlet kiss,
Then I could leave forever this abyss.
Dark poetess, sing to my heart the songs
For which my lonesome soul forever longs.

Sorcerer's Lament

I know the lore of wizard scrolls,
And grimoires rotted through with holes—
The only volume I've not read
Is that enshrined within your heart.

I know rare philters' recipes,
I'm master of lost alchemies—
The only potion I've not made
Is that which pairs us, unapart.

I know what shows the crystal ball,
Omniscient demons heed my call—
The only secret I can't see
Is that which glimmers in your soul.

I know the spells of wizards past,
And necromancies never cast—
The only charm not known to me
Is that of your caress' lull.

A Secret Sorcery

A secret sorcery
Into my heart has crept—
A serpent that has slept
Too long within my frozen soul
Has roused, and wrapped my heart,
And sunk in philtered fangs with cunning art.

A secret sorcery
Is blossoming within;
Slowly this rose has been
Opening scarlet petals full
Of wisps of pink perfume
That twine me like a succubus' doom.

A secret sorcery
Has taken me at last. . . .
A charming witch has cast
A spell to render her my sole
Desire and anodyne,
And I cannot but quaff of her dark wine.

Sorcerous Bond

For A. D.

Across the stars, the sorcerer and sorceress
    Were joined by a dark bond: the sorcerer spoke his plea
    In necromantic rhymes that echoed magickally
Across the moonlit night—and the witch answered yes.

Forevermore their bond is sealed, so mote it be.
    Enduring runes of scarlet flame their pact impress
    On parchments that the years cannot reduce to less—
Two dark hearts that one night twined in sweet wizardry.

The Scarlet Seal

For A. D.

O sorceress, my demon queen, my love divine,
    Will you renew the burning, necromantic vow
    So darkly taken by a moon-drunk midnight now
A year agone, a gem in Memory's golden shrine?

O sorceress, my seraph sapphire-eyed and fair,
    Press on my lips the cryptic seal your lips contain—
    That passionate seal of searing scarlet!—seal again
Your promise to be mine, no other love to share.

Lunar Love

For A. D.

Twelve moons have come and gone, my treasured sorceress,
    Since first we wrought the magick sigil of our love,
    Yet every ivory moon that since has passed above
Has lent to it a lunar rime—a fixedness.

But do not think this rime imparts an iciness;
    For under crystal layers hardened by each moon,
    Our sigil still lies hot, each figure, every rune,
Still burning like a ruby brand—extinguishless.

Dark Valentine

For A. D.

One night of crimson witchery I wrote a rune
    To you that asked if you'd be my dark valentine;
    You penned a purple spell that said you would be mine—
And ah, my heart was borne by daemons over the moon!

But you were only mine for one enchanted day—
    Or so I thought; the stars had other plans for us.
    Now I am asking you to be my succubus—
My Queen of waking dreams that never fade away.

Love Atlantean

I loved you in Atlantis long ago. . . .
Princess and bard were we—have you forgot
How by a sunset of ripe apricot
We watched the purple tide heap pearls, and go?
I made you rhymes of your charms manifold;
You hearkened close, with breathless rapture taut;
And when my words died in the waves' soft sough,
You drowned me in your locks of tangled gold.

I loved you long ago. . . . How have your eyes
Become so strange, so distant, and so cold?
They gaze upon me as through ocean deeps,
Lingering sadly on a dream that dies.
Our love is drowned amid the treasure-keeps
Of lost Atlantis, nevermore to rise,
Save in the foam-fine memories where it sleeps.

To an Unknown Enchantress

I know not in what land or time you are,
Nor have I known the cantrip of your name,
Nor the invultuation of your voice,
Nor the pervading spikenard of your skin,
Nor the enchantment of your magick touch;
But of your eyes I've known the witchery
A time or two . . . twin runes that render lame
All of my will, and that cause to rejoice
Against its gyves the daemon held within,
And that brand on my heart an ebon blotch—
A wound for which you are sole remedy.

I know not in what land or time you are,
But if you chance to read this rotted scroll
By crimson light from skies of dying earth,
When an abyss of stars will yawn to glut
Itself on all of Beauty, Hope, and Love,
Eat of the dwale that nods above my grave,
Fed on a heart long claimed by death and dole,
Yet where a rosy coal defying dearth
Of life endures; and your eyes softly shut;
And lie you down upon my grave, and prove
That you would love me where black wavelets lave.

Beneath the Cold, Cold Stars

For A. D.

Beneath the cold, cold stars I kissed my love,
    Ere we each went our own benighted way;
    O how I ached in her warm arms to stay—
But I could not with such cruel skies above.

A million stars all shimmered in her eyes
    As from her arms I slipped to face the night.
    A single tear, a drop of silver light,
Slipped down her moon-pale cheek, a star that dies.

Whole galaxies were quenched within that tear,
    Drowned in the river of oblivion—
    But these were naught beside the violet sun
Of love which strove against the stars' cold leer.

The Perishing Rose

For A. D.

Lastly the rose must perish in the shadows of an autumn eve,
    Obliviously wilting as its petals blow across the lawn,
    Vaporing dreams of crimson death until its smoldering soul is
    gone,
Escaped to perfume faerie groves awhile ere it forever leave. . . .

Yet though it perish, you and I shall walk a carpet wonderful,
    Of fragrant crimson petals, as we stroll the pleasance hand in
    hand,
    United in the twilight, traveling through love's enchanted land,
And treading feathered footsteps, lest we break a spell so beautiful.

Decapitated Kiss

Locked in our stocks, the heavy blades above,
    I take one final, longing look at you,
    Your moon-fair face, your twilight eyes of blue,
Your raven mane the night is jealous of.

The crowd is quiet, still they will not dare
    To ridicule, or look us in the eyes—
    They fear our power, knowing it unwise
To mock a witch, lest curses taint the air.

The priest recites our sins, we whisper spells
    To kill the crops for all the wrongs they've done;
    We will not deal them death, but dim the sun,
So that a shadow stains their asphodels.

And when we finish breathing forth our blight,
    And we each wait our guillotine's swift stroke,
    One final wish within me is awoke—
That I could kiss you for one last delight.

My wizard will ensures our lips won't miss.
    Into this basket both our heads will fall,
    And while our eyes yet gaze through death's black pall,
We'll share a last, decapitated kiss.

Love Beyond the Grave

On Halloween, when from the Otherworld
The dead are granted one night to return
To living lands, where guiding candles burn,
I visit my belovèd golden-curled.
I watch her weeping through the windowpane,
Her pallid features all with teardrops pearled;
She lays a crimson rose before my urn,
Dreaming of daggers and an end to pain.

Alas, how soon, my love, I must depart,
Not to return until next year! In vain
I strive against the Veil, although my heart
Loves from beyond the grave, with wizard art.
And yet as I am drawn back to the land
Of death and dream, through forests grave and grand—
I feel familiar fingers take my hand.

Love Beyond the Grave

Graveyard Promise

My love,
I have gone down at last unto the grave.
Above,
I hear you weeping where the flowers wave,
Tears offered to the love you could not save.

The rose
You place so gently on my twilight plot
Soon blows,
Its petals strown amongst the weeds to rot—
But our love, my love, shall never be forgot.

THE PALACE OF PHANTASIES

Cemetery of Broken Hearts

Where broken hearts lie buried in the mold,
    Leaking dead loves that nourish sickly vines,
    Which slither serely over weathered signs
Of names inscribed on tombstones cracked of old,

A lambent witch-fire charms the darkling air—
    An elfin spell of ghostly, golden lights,
    Wherein the sportful courtship of two sprites
Is all that stirs the haunted stillness there.

The Corpse of Beauty

Upon her bier of stone,
Her gorgeous corpse receives the night,
Her face a second softly shining moon.
With leaves of seasons flown
Her raven tresses are bedight,
Across cold granite lying lifeless strewn.

Her sightless, sapphire eyes
Stare through a maze of arbor boughs
At ghosts of stars extinguished long ago.
Her soul among them flies,
An argent star no night can douse,
A lonely lantern lending lonely glow.

Held to her breast, a rose
Whose bloody folds betray the taint
Of putrefaction's black and reptant blight.
Within that crimson close,
Corruption spreads to Quiet's plaint,
In lieu of chewing her inviolate white.

But even now the flower
Is barely more than brittle thorns,
And soon her beauty must begin to rot.
So Faerieland I'll scour—
Beyond its last, enchanted bourns—
To find that rarest rose so often sought.

And having plucked my prize,
I'll hasten to her resting place
And lay upon her breast the fabled bloom.
And in those sapphire eyes
I'll gaze on scenes of vanished grace,
Wherein I'll find my final, peaceful doom.

Moonrise

An amber orb, the sun fell in the west,
As on a pyre of flames empyreal;
The moon, an orb of chalcedony, rose
From eastern mist to start her skyward quest.

Half indistinct in far-off azure dream,
She clomb a vault not yet sidereal,
Doffing a cloak of gray haze to disclose
To all her naked beauty, white, supreme.

Hovering over the horizon far,
So hesitant on stairs aetherial,
She cast a gaze so longing, lachrymose,
Straight at the sun, like parting lovers share.

Upon her solemn, cold, and pallid cheek,
There mirrored was a smile imperial;
She bore this brand—most bright of all her woes—
Up to the stars, sad solitude to seek.

The Moonward Trail

I choose the mystic, moonward trail
    As crickets chirp their vesper hymn,
    And shadows down each hillside swim.
Behind, the falling sun will fail—
I choose the mystic, moonward trail.

It winds between the drowsy hills
    In shade of lone and ancient trees,
    The haunts of hidden faëries.
Far off, aloof, the half-moon wills
Me onward toward the drowsy hills.

Realms magical must surely dream
    Beyond the endless, dusking blue
    Horizon the moon draws me to. . . .
Past hills that half fantastic seem,
This trail must lead to lands of dream.

But nightfall means I must turn back.
    A cold wind blasts my slow return,
    And sunset lances blind and burn.
—But moonward flees the elfin track,
And yearning fancy must turn back.

Possibilities

What gnome might dwell within the ancient tree?
    What unicorn might grace the tranquil glade?
    What witch might haunt the woodland's tangled shade?
—These are the questions Fancy asks of me.

Faerie Song

Come away through wood and field,
  Come away down hidden glen,
Where the cool brook flows concealed
  Toward a dim land hid from men. . . .

Tarry not too long, O mortal!
  Tarry not whilst beckon we!
For you cannot pass the Portal,
  Save if brought by faërie.

Hasten not so quick, O mortal!
  Hasten not without a care!
We are fickle!—none can foretell
  If you would return from there.

Come away through wood and field,
  Come away down hidden glen;
Come or stay, your fate is sealed—
  For we shall not meet again.

The Faerie Moon

But once a century, by dying year,
    When swirling wind collects its branch-borne tithe—
    When trees autumnal madly sway and writhe—
An emerald moon mounts swollen, pale and clear!

A weird green witch-fire glimmers in the air,
    Like shaken light from limpid, rippling pools;
    And all the swards erupt with white toadstools;
And wanton laughter flutters everywhere. . . .

From out the woods glide fays that print no tracks,
    Each one a tiny Venus lily-white,
    With elfin features, tresses flower-bedight
Unkemptly falling over hollow backs.

They join their hands inside a faerie-ring,
    And dance their round, a wheel of tangling knees;
    And chant ecstatic lunar litanies;
And fan the fervor of their faerie fling!

The emerald shine is glory on their breasts!
    The emerald shimmer in their hair is bliss!
    The emerald fire is on their flesh a kiss!
They heed their emerald passions' green behests. . . .

All this beneath the emerald Faerie Moon
    That rises only once a century,
    Compelling all the creatures of the Sidhe
To roam once more. . . . And its next rise is soon.

Duel with the Dark Double

From out the moonshade of a tree,
   My doppelgänger stepped:
A phantom black as death was he,
   And on my path he kept.

I drew my sword, its argent glowed,
   Surcharged by aegis moon;
He drew his shadow-sword, and showed
   He meant to battle soon.

He waited there, a sentinel
   Upon the forking path:
As if by sympathetic spell,
   I shared his cunning wrath.

I started with a fell attack,
   To seek an instant kill—
But lunar silver clashed with black,
   And rang with thwarted will.

He blocked my each and every blow,
   And parried I in turn;
I did the death-dance with my foe,
   But none felt steel's cold burn.

We wove a labyrinth of swords,
    Clanging grim symphonies;
Of night and combat we were lords,
    Urged by black goeties.

But still he mirrored every move—
    We were a perfect pair
Of puppets, as if just above
    Twin hands worked this nightmare.

I stopped dead still, he halted too,
    Each sword a waiting snake;
I knew then what I was to do,
    What victory would take.

I lashed out with a sudden strike,
    A move I'd never tried:
It pained him and surprised alike
    When steel slid through his side.

I followed with a swift assault
    Of wild and new attacks,
Each one a lunar lightning-bolt—
    My foe could not relax.

Each killing cut sprayed spirit-flame,
    A purple phantom fire
That lit our deadly midnight game,
    A dying demon's pyre.

I knew then that my twin was doomed,
    And with a slaying slash
I clove his neck, and from it fumed
    A plume of purple ash.

The headless fiend sunk to his knees,
    His sword dissolved away;
His corpse was scattered on the breeze,
    As ash with leaves a-stray.

And so I strode into the night,
    Upon my chosen road.
Unhindered by my shadow-wight,
    My pathway plainly showed.

I walked beneath the cobalt moon,
    My sword hung at my side,
My double's charred remains far-strewn,
    My crimson cloak flung wide.

Nocturnal Flowers

Nocturnal flowers open in the night,
    Unfurling petals lush and velvet black,
    Which breathe a dream-spiced perfume that, alack,
Is lost in violet steam to stars' far light.

The Well of Purple Wine

Upon the planet's outer rim,
Guarded by stellar teraphim,
There was a well where I would drink,
Whilst pondering the blue-starred brink
Of space infinite, scintillant
With worlds like motes—the firmament
Was like a cloud of wizard dust,
Dispersed by interstellar gust.

When first I lowered down the pail
Of planished silver, set with pale
Opals, I drew up purple wine,
Whereon there sparkled starry shine.
I quaffed its contents, and descried
On distant stars that lurked outside
My former sight, perspectives weird
And wondrous wheresoever I peered. . . .

But then there came the evil day
When water drowned each starry ray.
I drank and drank, but still my eyes
Could fathom not the chasmal skies.
But still I drank, till only sand
In mocking slithered through my hand,
Blown starward by a sudden gust
Of demon wind, like mummy dust.

Zeriatis

O Zeriatis, outermost of stars,
Who flame your rosy phare against the Night,
Alone before Oblivion's dreadful might,
Have I not known in other avatars
Your perfumed pathways, spanning endless miles
Of gardens strewn with shrines of malachite,
Upon whose plinths the eidolons of Lars
Greet worshipers with only cryptic smiles . . . ?

I fain would walk once more your twilight ways,
By light of scarlet lamps that light those aisles
And idol-guarded glades against the days
That dim beneath a shroud no god would raise.
But even as I gaze upon your glow,
Farthest of stars that only dreamers know,
Your light has died . . . and I am filled with woe.

The Dreamer

I am a dreamer . . . little do you know
Of what unfolds behind my lidded eyes.
You have not peered upon the violet skies
Where Zeriatis burns with ruby glow.
Nor have you braved the perilous path through Yph,
The foggy wood where fangèd orchids rise
To bite the dreamer who should walk too slow,
Becoming drunker with each perfumed whiff. . . .

For had you traveled those dim ways of dream,
And conquered every gem-encrusted cliff
Of Mount Vaethmyrra, whereon manticores
And other strange, unnamed chimaeras teem—
Then you would reign behind these golden doors,
Within this crystal castle, whose bright gleam
With brilliance of three moons forever wars.

The Dreamer

Writing Shrine

(On a practice feverishly observed and advocated by
    the mad poet D. L. Myers)

Upon my desk I keep a strange array
    Of curious objects that ensorcel me—
    Gargoyles and gemstones, things of wizardry,
Which serve to keep the mundane world at bay.

Oracle of the Black Pool

For D. L. Myers

Deep in a wood whose stagnant, nauseous gloom
Hides death behind each twitching, serrate leaf,
There lies a pool in whose dark mirror loom
Huge yellow flowers drooling liquid kief—
A poison sap that makes a sirup dire
Out of the pool, its verge a graveyard weird.
And like a lichen mid the floral fire,
There droops a dripping, sallow-stainèd beard. . . .

The Oracle from out the Black Pool sips,
And mutters madness to the twisting trees.
For coin or gem, from out his trembling lips
Whisper will he of things no sane man sees. . . .
But be you warned, who seeks that shriveled ghoul—
His visions are more lethal than the Pool!

The Wrath of Xyre

For D. L. Myers

O Oracle, you tempt the wrath of Xyre.
    Your scrolls of venomed runes are overlate.
    My waning patience grows as delicate
As rotting roses in the dying year.

The icy moon enrimes you with its doom,
    A creeping chill which chains you to the grave;
    And every dark star glitters like a glaive,
Lethal with death borne from the farthest gloom.

The blackest spells in grimoires manifold
    Are rising in the raspy throats of wraiths
    Within my thrall. All Gods and magick faiths
Would each one fail to curb my wrath untold.

Hell's darkest demons hearken to my call,
    And astral alastors heed my command;
    And by a damning motion of my hand,
They would descend, unstayed by ward and wall.

I have prepared a pentagram to sear
    Your mortal soul with runes of violet death.
    Breathe carefully your every feeble breath,
For you have stirred the sateless wrath of Xyre.

The Wizard

In caverns lit with violet flames,
A wizard calls demonic names,
Which banish storms of bats accustomed to dark things,
Which flee on fearful wings.

The crimson tome from which he reads
Is writ in crimson script that bleeds.
The magick-kindled torches waver at the verse
That echoes like a curse.

Two golden candleholders, wrought
Like twisting serpents that have caught
Within their fangèd mouths infernal embers, blaze,
Beside a skull's dark gaze.

Spirit-possessed, the mantic skull,
With ghostly grave-light glowing full,
Recites a recipe an ancient alchemist
Had thought unwise to list.

The wizard stirs the cauldron wroth
With perfumed amaranthine froth—
A brew of rare ingredients from crystal jars,
Made dire by evil stars.

A wyvern, at the wizard's word,
Drops in the thing it has procured—
A squirming, screaming mandrake torn from a dark fen
Shunned by all mortal men.

Dipping his goblet in the brew,
The wizard sips and pales in hue. . . .
He sighs, and knows at last his deathless life is slain—
His search no more in vain.

Khayyam's Wine

Where is the wine Khayyam would have me quaff?
What sanguine grape will gush forth juice enough?
    And from what gilded cup, pray, should I sip?—
My dromedary I must soon fall off. . . .

Long have I traveled with this caravan,
Forsaking all the pleasures of Ispahan,
    But in no far-flung land have found to drip
The precious Vintage, since my quest began.

Omar Khayyam, have you no little wine
Yet left within your jug—that modest shrine
    For such a grand elixir?—Have you no
Single drop left that I, parched, might make mine?

"Alas, your search has been in vain, my friend—
And now your brief life falters nigh its end.
    In Ispahan my wine was wont to flow—
But you perceived not where the Grape did pend.

"My wine you might have tasted by the stream
With golden sunlight gorgeously agleam;
    The Vintage might have inked the book of verse
You might have read beside it, deep in dream.

"Some perfect houri's lips, the cup wherefrom
You might have drained its dregs, thereat to plumb
    Pleasures yet deeper hid in passion's purse,
Amid warm limbs . . . to which wise men succumb.

"You might have wrung it from the hanging notes
Adrift in dazzling courts where lute-song floats;
    You might have found it in a spring-fed bath,
Enfolden in the fragile, moon-white lotes.

"You might have traveled to the sapphire stars
On stairs of censer-smoke, unstayed by bars;
    And might you have, along your cosmic path,
Drained from the Crescent's cup wine pressed from Mars!

"In aromatic marts my wine was sold,
Its dye in every Persian rug unrolled,
    Its rich bouquet, olibanum and myrrh
Mingled with song and laughter thousandfold.

"In garden-close where sings the nightingale,
Among the rose you might have made wassail;
    And trysting with the Sultan's consorts there
Well might have made the Wine rise, red and hale. . . .

"But you forsook all this for sighing sand,
Thinking to find my wine in some far land.
    Cocaigne has lain before your purblind eyes—
You knew it not when there your feet did stand.

"I see you slipping from your camel's back,
Weighed down by more than just your travel-pack.
    I have a draught for you, my friend, who hies
Horizonward, and never shall turn back.

"Questioned you not the specters at your side,
Whom this strange eve with you began to ride?
    And have you never wondered where may lead
This caravan's black-cloaked, scythe-sceptered guide?

"Here, sate your thirst, my friend, here, one last drink
Before the sun in shadowed dunes should sink.
    Now, at the last, by this black wine be freed—
Here is the jug Death gave me, do not shrink."

Lord of Illusion

Prismatic walls of splendor rear at my command,
More tenuous than air, but thick with visions fair.
Peer not too deep into the dreams wrought by my wand,
For all too soon they fade and leave doomed hearts dismayed.

The Palace of Phantasies

I have a little time upon my couch to lie;
    Therefore this eve I give unto the vagaries—
    The purple phantasies—
Of my imagination's daemon, soaring high
On fragrant censer smoke and my escaping sigh,
    Ennui awhile to ease.

Enthroned on crimson cushions deep with pillows piled,
    Encrowned with drowsiness, I rule a dim demesne
    Where opium, not pain,
Presides over a palace opulent, enisled
By suffering and sadness, yet still undefiled
    By their besieging stain.

But now a hushed unrest has crept into its halls;
    Voices of evil hiss behind each arras fair;
    Vermiculate, the vair;
The shadows cast by candles spread like creeping palls;
The chalice wherefrom I would quaff rare magistrals
    Conium seems to bear.

Even into my deepest keep a plague pursues—
    Even up to the crowning tower's highest heights.
    I tire of the delights
Illusory in which I thought myself to lose;
My house of spectral pleasures quakes as Boredom brews—
    For whims the worst of blights.

I sit as king within a crumbling empery,
    Abandoned by my subjects, facing monstrous doom,
    My marble throne, my tomb.
Too soon the towers builded so fantastically
Against my worldly weariness descend with me
    Through dead and dreamless gloom.

I wake upon my crimson couch—the hour is late;
    The censer is extinguished, and its coals are cold
    Within its figured gold.
Alas, my daemon listless lies where once it sate
With wings outspread to prove the vesper's violet gate—
    Which now no more unfold.

TWILIGHT SORROWS

The Tree

The ancient tree,
It talks to me,
In woeful whispers
Over the lea. . . .
In violet vespers,
Black-silhouetted,
Its boughs, star-netted,
Cast witchery.

Outside the pane,
A sad refrain
Sighs in its branches,
Full of pain;
And nothing stanches
The crimson weeping
Of leaves a-leaping
In winds insane.

Our souls entwine,
The tree's and mine;
I share its sadness,
With it pine—
We mourn the gladness
Of springs departed,
As night, sad-hearted,
Pours bitter wine.

Autumn Hearts

The autumn trees are hung with hearts,
    All shriveled, shrunken, atrophied:
    They beat and moribundly bleed,
And shake as each new soul departs.

Their torpid pulses, sick and sad,
    But scarce remember vernal years,
    As rattling in cold wind that seres,
They weakly cling to all they had.

Toadstools

Emerging from beneath the crimson rot
    Of autumn's tattered dress, the white toadstools
    Rear like the dwarfèd heads of fungal ghouls
That feast upon a corpse that time forgot.

October

Dark time of death, and dreams, and haunted skies,
    When trees contort in twisted agony—
When sereing wind so miserably cries—
When all of joy in scarlet tatters lies—
When far-off mists of sorrow witch my eyes,
    And all is strange with autumn gramarye.

October lingers near the year's gray tomb
    As jack-o'-lanterns cackle wickedly—
As crucified in cornfields, scarecrows loom—
As crow-caws echo through obscuring brume—
As I embrace the specter-shrouded gloom,
    And all my soul knows sad tranquility.

All Hallow's Eve

A wraith of eld goes wandering this night,
    From out hesternal autumns, through the mist,
Lonely and lost, its only guiding light
    A single coal that hell has hardly missed.

So too the youth I was so long ago
    Goes off to wander through a phantom past,
Whose jack-o'-lanterns still yet faintly glow
    Amid dim dreams that sadly could not last.

Jack-o'-Lanterns

The jack-o'-lanterns gather in October
    As Halloween on vampire pinions nears.
From every porch with autumn shadows sober,
    They cast their crooked, silent-cackling leers.

As orange eve is drowned in violet twilight,
    And every tree lifts darkling tracery,
The jack-o'-lanterns, all with hell-lent coals, light
    The way of wraiths that wander mournfully.

Their flaming faces foulder on the blackness
    Like visages of ghouls in Erebus.
The jack-o'-lanterns light the windy darkness,
    And watch the leaves trace pathways tortuous.

The Wraith

Last Halloween at twilight strange and gray,
As haunted winds told tales of yesterday,
And crimson leaves blew on their aimless way,
    As from an unseen door,
From out the woods a wraith, grave-visaged, old,
Draped in a hooded robe hard to behold,
Came forth to seek amid the windy cold
    Some way it knew of yore.

At night it wandered through the ancient town,
All wrapped in fog, a huge and ghostly gown.
It found at last the house nigh crumbling down:
    Outside, a lonesome flame
Had drawn it forth from death to seek again,
For just one night, a life mid mortal men—
But something seemed to vex the spirit then—
    Something was not the same.

Where as of old a candle's guiding light
Would welcome home the wraith from autumn night—
A jack-o'-lantern grinned in cruel delight,
    And seared it with despair!
Its woeful features crumbled from its face,
Leaving a screaming skull to take their place.
And of that wraith of eld soon not a trace
    Was left on misty air.

Thin Grows the Veil

Thin grows the Veil. . . . A hush hangs over all.
Not a leaf twitches in the windless air,
Which glows with autumn gold, soft, mystical,
Seeming to fade, as in an aether rare.
Betimes the final twilight will descend,
Like to a cerecloth on the dying Year,
Who lies beneath a catafalque of tall
Black trees whose boughs above her sadly bend.

But as she dies, the olden dead return
As wraiths that through the dusk-witched meadows wend,
All through this Hallow's Even to sojourn
Among the living, free from grave and urn.
And maybe next year's autumn, when once more
The Portal opens, days beyond death's door
Will come again, in ghostly state of yore.

November

You've come again, O gray November—
Come to quench the brume-dim ember
Of a sun that would remember
    Summer days dissolved in mist.

The smoke of candles long extinguished
Chokes your skies, and indistinguished
Loom the trees of autumn, languished,
    In gray leagues of dole abyssed.

Red leaves rain down, crows take their places,
But your hush allows no traces
Of their calls—the silence cases
    All as in a monstrous tomb.

You've come again, O gray November—
Come to stoke the dreaming ember
Of a soul whose corpse-light amber
    Glows more bright in deathly gloom.

Funereal Sun

A sickly witch-fire in the murky sky,
    The sun shines feebly through a funeral shroud
    Of endless dismal, gray, cadaverous cloud,
Like the wan face of one that soon will die.

Winter Crow

Atop a withered tree,
Enrobed in mourning black,
The winter crow observes its bleak demesne:
Below, the dismal lea;
Above, no sunny crack
Divides the clouds—and silence broods between.

Unto the misty air,
It screams its raspy call—
A dirge for all things dead and once held dear.
Into vague branches bare,
And twilight's distant pall,
It echoes off to die with yesteryear.

Twilight Sorrows

Now is the time when twilight weaves its spell
Of pensive purple through my spirit. . . .
The sun is tombed beyond the blackened fell,
My heart has no more light to cheer it.
Not quite the same that sun will rise tomorrow,
Now is the hour of twilight sorrow.

Now is the time when every wistful sigh
Combines to sweep like broom-sped witches
Through rattling trees that claw the bruising sky,
Like hands of maggot-anguished liches.
I fear the torment that will come tomorrow,
Now is the hour of twilight sorrow.

Now is the time when stars burn icily
In the black vault that swallows heaven—
Each one the corpse-light of a memory
Of things of which I am bereaven.
For yesterday I wish, receive tomorrow,
Now is the hour of twilight sorrow.

Now is the time when crickets keen for all
That served to stack the sunset's pyre;
Their song is sweetly sad, funereal,
And sets my soul with pain afire.
There will be naught but ash to sift tomorrow,
Now is the hour of twilight sorrow.

The Angels All Are Corpses in the Sky

The angels all are corpses in the sky,
    Interred within the wide, black tomb of night;
And every white star is a cold, dead eye
    Set in a rotting face that has no sight.

With withered wings impressively outspread—
    Albeit in death-posture impotence—
The mummied angels loom as shapes of dread,
    With starry stares unblinking, cold, intense.

All human prayers drift past their heedless ears—
    Which could not hear even were they free of worms—
Each one a whisper that soon disappears
    In yawning chaos, tossed by stellar storms.

Their horrid faces haunt the starry vault,
    Whenever I dare to lift one fearful eye.
Sometimes immersed in desperate prayer, I halt—
    The angels all are corpses in the sky.

The Angels All Are Corpses in the Sky

The Mascaron

I peered in contemplation at a mascaron
    Whose anguished gaze entreated me
    To solve its mystery—
The doom that it endured, forever wrought in stone.

Its view would please the eye forever: here a place
    Where bloomed the amaranth and rose—
    A magic garden-close
Alive with drunken butterflies fragile as lace. . . .

Why then the horror written on its goatish brow?
    What scream caught in that leafy beard?
    Was ivy what it feared?—
The slow advance of vines that would no view allow?

No, no—it was not this that made the mask assume
    Its nightmare-tortured countenance,
    Its hollow, haunted glance—
Its only doom was but to bear the face of doom.

The Gargoyle

Perched high atop the ancientmost of towers,
    Enisled amid a dreamful sea of cloud,
    The agèd gargoyle, sad and lone and proud,
In stillness and in silence bides the hours.

With none but pigeons for rare company,
    And funeral tolls to rouse its granite heart,
    Pensive, it contemplates the rosy art
With which the sunset paints its empery.

With tears of rain, and silent, tortured howls,
    The stone grotesque laments its lonesome lot—
    A doom undreamed by even those who rot
In lower hell's most miserable bowels.

Down from that heaven-verging Tartarus
    It knows its volant wings will never fly—
    Until the tower crumbles down to die,
And the Abyss yawns wide, victorious.

Shattered Hopes

Too oft my hopes have fallen to the nadir of despair,
    That black, unyielding floor that founds the deepest pit of hell.
They lie in crystal shards that shine not in the lightless air,
    Till blindly feeling demons take them—where, I cannot tell.

Ancientness

The weight of many hundred ancient years
Bears down on me like dirt upon the dead;
And haze like cobwebs cataracts my eyes;
And dust of eld escapes my weary sighs.
My heart of parchment, faintly beating, tears,
And ashes pour whence living blood once bled.

Yet I live onward with a shriveled heart,
From which my stagnant soul hissed long ago,
And bear a burden greater than the grave—
The incubus of life that will not leave.
So through these latter ages must I chart
A course unending and weighed down with woe.

In Mortal Dream

I spill my blood upon the graves,
    Oblations to the dead.
    The weeds of centuries are red
With life death dimly craves.

This offering shall serve to wake
    The shades that slumber here,
    Beneath cracked tomb and lichened bier
Half lost in forest brake.

Rise ashen wraith and specter black,
    Rise newborn from my blood.
    You have more life than ever I could,
So live and look not back.

Now I must lie among the weeds
    So earth can take me home.
    In mortal dream let phantoms roam,
But sleep I now must needs.

The Doom of Words

Grimoire and volumen, stone tablet, tome,
    Line endless shelves, in archives veiled with Night—
    Retrieveless, save by skeleton and wight,
Which down those aisles in silence deathward roam.

It is the doom of words to molder there—
    No text immortal is to sateless Time.
    Mayhap some wraith will read my dusty rhyme
While stumbling down oblivion's ebon stair.

TRIBUTES

For K. A. Opperman

Twisted Trails of Thought

By Ashley Dioses

Amid the shadows of a tavern brightly lit,
Where boastful bards are singing horrid songs with wit,
There sits a silent bard alone, who sips his drink
While contemplating how those poetasters stink. . . .

Unlike those bards who sing their songs of bygone valor—
Ardent, with reddened cheeks—this bard of spectral pallor
Inscribes in blood so sinister a literature
Of such nefandous depths, and yet of such allure.

Deep twisted trails of thought stream through his darksome mind,
Full of cacodemonic tales, and spells that bind.
A fresh, alluring corpse, a lovely, ruined heart—
These fill the caverns of his soul and never part.

The blackest thoughts course through his magick fingertips,
And through his ceremonial work, nightmare soon grips.
His dark and intricate delights are spells he crafts,
Which summon shivers and cold shakes from more than drafts.

His art boasts of itself without the need for speech—
His poems touch deep places that so few can reach.
Such weaker bards all harbor secret fear of him;
Their thoughts, in public, never could be quite so grim.

A Sorcerous Tome

By Ashley Dioses

In my one mirror, I am not all I can see.
With blackest goeties ingrained in every vein,
I often scry upon its polished glass and gain
A glimpse of my dark Sorcerer, with book on knee.

He often is engrossed in his old Crimson Tome—
A tome of sorceries—of strange unknowns and lore—
Of mystic incantations, poems, spells, and more.
My wonder grows each time I see it in his home.

The Crimson Kist

By D. L. Myers

In dark and distant ages past,
    When blood-red oceans crashed upon
    Grim onyx spires before the dawn,
And strange wrack that the breakers cast,

Above the ebon-pebbled shore,
    A kist lay glinting crimson-bright,
    Aflame with rising ruby light,
A thing of otherworldly lore.

Inside its sparkling carmine womb,
    A crimson tome of mystic runes
    That speak of dread and sanguine moons
Aspin within the blackest tomb.

The Sorcerous Scribe

By D. L. Myers

Upon his naked bed of stone,
The darkling scribe, with furrowed brow,
Does dream of vistas silent, lone,
And drownèd shores Atlantean.

In crooked garret darkly cast
Of murky boulders stacked askew,
He conjures rhymes and verses vast
To crystallize the Muse's song.

The winds that whistle through the stones
To him speak words of burning cold,
Whilst terrors from black inner zones
Course from his stylus Gorgon-clasped.

Each cryptic motion of his hand
Magics mad beauty into being,
As phantoms from a jeweled land
Of faery and empyrean spheres.

So hail, dark scribe! fill up our skulls
With opalescent vistas past;
The crimson wine that smites and lulls,
And hands us all oblivion.

Acknowledgments

"Witch's Charms," "Nocturnal Flower," "To an Unknown Enchantress," "Sorcerer's Lament" (as "Cantrip"), "Decapitated Kiss," "Duel with the Dark Double," "The Corpse of Beauty," "A Heart Defiled," "Mandrake," "Soul Rot," and "Succubus" appeared in *Dark River Press* (1st quarter 2012).

"Dark Poetry" and "Dark Star of My Desire" appeared in *Horrotica* (December 2012).

"The Faerie Moon," "The Wraith," and "Blood" appeared in the *Horror Zine* (August 2013).

"Nocturnal Poet," "Siren of the Dead," and "The Angels All Are Corpses in the Sky" appeared in *Spectral Realms* (July 2014).

www.ingramcontent.com/pod-product-compliance
Lightning Source LLC
Chambersburg PA
CBHW071219090426
42736CB00014B/2889